Jersey Wooly Rabbits

The Pet Guide for Jersey Wooly Rabbits

Jersey Wooly Rabbits General Info, Purchasing, Care, Marketing, Keeping, Health, Supplies, Food, Breeding and More Included!

By Lolly Brown

Foreword

Jersey Woolies, also known as the "no – kick" bunnies, are one of the most docile and popular rabbit breeds in United States. As a crossbreed of a French Angora and a Netherland Dwarf rabbit, this cute little bunch inherited many physical traits from its parent breed that makes it suitable as family pets. The easy – to – care coat of Jersey Woolies as well as its miniature size are the major reasons why many people choose this rabbit breed. It is also the factors why this new breed was recognized by many rabbit registries and why it became a hit among rabbit enthusiasts.

But even if Jersey Woolies are great looking pets, it may not be the right choice for everyone so before you decide whether or not it might be the right companion for you, why not take the time to learn more about this breed? In this book you will get to learn general information about the Jersey Wooly including its biological background, physical attributes, how to keep it healthy, how to groom it, how to breed and sell it as well as habitat maintenance and proper husbandry.

Table of Contents

Introduction

Jersey Wooly or also commonly referred to as "mug head" is a dwarf rabbit breed type with a relatively small face with short hairs on it that distinguishes them from almost similar looking rabbit breeds like the Angora species and the Netherland Dwarf rabbits (though they are the result of this crossbreeds). The ears are also short but erect, and its fluff goes through their whole body. This breed is usually identified by the type of their wools. Jersey Woolies usually possess light fluffy wool, dense wool or sort of coarse wool that pretty much looks like a human hair when it is laid down and flat throughout the breed's body. Its bold head, bright eyes, fluffy appearance and its square type face plus its affectionate breed is what makes the Jersey Wooly one of the most popular rabbit breed as pets.

According to most breeders and rabbit enthusiasts, Jersey Woolies are very playful, sweet and also docile. They can be laid back lap bunnies, outdoor explorers or someone you can really enjoy as a house companion. They pretty much get along with other rabbit breeds as well as other household pets such as cats and dogs provided that there is proper introduction. They respond well to training, and tend to also enjoy the company of strangers.

Even if the Jersey Woolies' fur or coat seems quite hard to maintain, in reality, they are relatively easy to groom even though it is quite dense in texture. Aside from the general information, biological background, and physical attributes of Jersey Wooly rabbits, this book will also delve deeper on how to take care of Jersey Wooly in terms of its health, nutrition, grooming, habitat, and husbandry.

You will also be informed about how to breed them, learn the criteria for showing and showmanship guidelines as well as some marketing tips should you choose to become a rabbit raiser. Pros and cons will also be provided as well as some links to resources that can help you to better understand this cute bunny with a great personality wrapped up in a small package!

Chapter One: Biological Information

Jersey Woolies perfect rabbit pets for those living in apartments, for first time rabbit keepers, for families with children and even for senior citizens! Although this rabbit breed is generally easy to care for, it may not be the right choice for everyone so before you deciding to buy a Jersey Wooly or any rabbit breed for this matter, why not get enough knowledge first about these species and learn what they are really all about? In this chapter you will receive an introduction to the breed including some basic biological facts and general information as well as the history of how it came about.

Taxonomy, Origin and History

The Jersey Wooly has a scientific name of *Oryctolagus cuniculus*. They belong in Kingdom *Animalia*, Phylum *Chordata*, Class *Mammalia*, Order *Lagomorpha*, Family *Leporidae*, and Genus *Oryctolagus*.

Jersey Wooly is a crossbreed of a French Angora rabbit and Netherland Dwarf rabbits. They were primarily intended as a pet trade. However, this cute little bunny became more than just a rabbit developed for pet trading purposes only because eventually it became popular and was also widely known as the "no – kick" bunny.

Around 1970 to 1980, many rabbit breeders tried to develop small breeds or dwarf type of rabbits. During this time, there were a lot of new rabbit breeds that became a member of the largest rabbit registry in the United States which is the American Rabbit Breeders Association (ARBA).

The Jersey Wooly were crossbred by a woman in New Jersey named Bonnie Seeley, and the breed was officially introduced in 1984 to the ARBA with the hopes of creating a dwarf rabbit that has an easy to groom wool coat. Seeley produced a breed to the size and body type she wanted and then presented it for the first time in Florida during the ARBA convention. After four years of careful selection, the

ARBA officially recognized the breed, and it instantly became one of the most popular rabbit household pets. The Jersey Wooly also became a widely – exhibited rabbit during rabbit shows at that time.

After a few years, the Jersey Wooly became an instant hit and was included as one of the ten most popular rabbit show breed. The main advantage of having a Jersey Wooly as a pet is that its coat is very easy to clean and daily grooming is not required compared to most rabbit breeds like an American fuzzy lop. Just a quick brush will do and perhaps the only thing that owners should watch out is the wool block but other than that the Jersey Wooly is generally easy to care for.

Size, Life Span, and Physical Appearance

Jersey Woolies are small or dwarf size rabbits that weigh an average 1 to 3 pounds for both bucks and does, with 3 ½ pounds being the maximum senior weight. It stands at about 2 inches long, and its ears measure about 3 inches in length. The Jersey Wooly can only live up between 7 to 12 years or more depending on how you take care of its health. These bunnies have a small, compact body with erect ears, and roundish bright eyes. Its eyes are usually black, brown and red in color though there are also those who possess blue colored eyes. Jersey woolies have six color variations that are recognized by the ARBA.

They come in chestnut, squirrel color, chinchilla, opal, white, lilac, blue, chocolate, black, blue – eyed – white, red – eyed – white as well as a shaded group color that comes in smoke pearl, seal, Siamese sable, sable point tortoise shell, blue tortoise shell, black and blue otter, sable marten, lilac silver marten, black silver marten, and chocolate silver marten. It also comes in any other variety such as the pointed white black and the pointed white blue variety

One of their unique physical characteristics is of course their easy to brush wools that are soft, dense and sometimes coarse texture. Jersey Woolies are known as one of the most docile rabbit breeds, and has a gentle disposition. They are very easy to care for, very friendly household pets, and most of all a small rabbit breed that any newbie or expert can surely handle.

Jersey Wooly Temperament and Behavior

Jersey Wooly rabbits are naturally docile but very social creatures. Aside from hanging out with their human keepers, they also enjoy being kept with other rabbits. When it comes to acquiring more than one rabbit, it is not necessarily a requirement that you keep two of the same kind of rabbit either as long as they are similar in size and their cage provides ample space for both, you can keep as many Jersey Woolies as you want.

The best way to ensure harmony among your rabbits is to raise them together from a young age, ideally younger than twelve weeks. Two or more Jersey Wooly rabbits can be ideal but make sure that before you get another one, you can provide for the needs of both rabbits. If you keep more than two rabbits together, you also have to make sure that there is no more than one male for every two females. The best combination is an altered male and female pair or a pair of brothers or sisters.

Jersey Wooly and Other Pets

The tempers vary from one rabbit to another; some rabbits might be very docile and friendly like the Jersey Wooly but other breeds may be a little more nervous, aggressive or simply irrational.

When it comes to other household pets, you also have to consider the temperament of your dog or cat. Some pets have a very low prey drive so you don't really have to worry about them chasing your Jersey Wooly around although it is not recommended either since Jersey Woolies are dwarf size breeds. Terriers and other hunting breeds on the other hand may have a very high prey drive and if your rabbit has a high flight response, it could lead to a dangerous chase and could also be potentially stressful for your bunny.

The best thing to do is to introduce your pets to each other while they are still young so they can grow up together and get use to one another's behavior. But even so, you should still supervise their interactions to be safe.

Quick Facts

Origin: New Jersey, United States

Pedigree: crossbreed of French Angora and Netherland Dwarf rabbit

Breed Size: dwarf – size breed

Body Type and Appearance: Has a compact and small body with proportionate legs, bright round eyes, upright or erect ears, bold head and soft wool.

Group/s: American Rabbit Breeders Association, National Jersey Wooly Rabbit Club, British Rabbit Council, Australian National Rabbit Council

Height: stands at about 2 ½ inches

Weight: average of 1 – 3 pounds

Coat Length: short wooly coat

Coat Texture: soft, dense, coarse

Color: Agouti variation includes chestnut, squirrel color, chinchilla, and opal. Broken group include a white variation. Self – group colors including lilac, blue, chocolate, black, blue – eyed – white, and red – eyed – white. Shaded group colors such as smoke pearl, seal, Siamese sable, sable point tortoise shell, and blue tortoise shell. Tan pattern including black and blue otter, sable marten, lilac silver marten, black silver marten, and chocolate silver marten. It also comes in any other variety such as the pointed white black and the pointed white blue variety

Temperament: extremely docile, gentle, friendly, playful, sociable, trainable

Strangers: friendly around strangers

Other Rabbits: generally good with other rabbit breeds if properly introduced, trained, and socialized.

Other Pets: generally friendly with other pets but shouldn't be left with other huge animals because it might get scared since rabbits are mostly prey animals.

Exercise Needs: provide toys for mental and physical stimulation and a space they can roam around in.

Health Conditions: this rabbit breed is predisposed to common illnesses such as Sniffles Disease, Urine Scald, Abscesses, Pneumonia, Viral Hemorrhagic Disease (RVHD),

Infectious Myxomatosis, E. Cuniculi, Mange Mites, and Ringworm.

Lifespan: average 7 to 12 years or more

Chapter Two: The Rabbit Buying Process

Sometimes purchasing rabbits can be overwhelming especially for those who are first time rabbit breeders or keepers. If a rabbit enthusiast fails to buy a desired rabbit breed, like a Jersey Wooly for this matter, due to the fact that they the breed is not available at nearby pet shops or stores, they tend to purchase a pet that they will later regret. A lot of people don't even know where to buy which makes them vulnerable in purchasing a rabbit breed from irresponsible breeders or acquiring an unhealthy bunny.

If you are one of them, then this chapter is what you need before you start this journey with your potential rabbit. You'll learn where to buy, the pros and cons of those places as well as the criteria on how to spot a good and responsible rabbit breeder so that you can be assured that your pet is healthy and well taken care of.

Where to Purchase Rabbits?

There are several places where you can buy rabbits, and in this section we'll explain the pros and cons of buying from these places. You can buy from pet shops, flea markets, backyard rabbit breeders or private breeders, rabbit rescue centers, and from dedicated rabbit hobbyists.

Pet Shops

The most popular place to buy Jersey Wooly rabbits or any animal is of course from your local pet shops. And just like other popular pets like dogs, cats, birds, guinea pigs and the likes, rabbits are always available in most pet shops. However, most breeders do not recommend and in fact highly discourage people to purchase rabbits from these pet shops simply because the store owners don't know anything about particular rabbit breeds, and more often than not the animals sold in pet shops are not being properly taken care of. They're probably selling or breeding rabbits for the sole purpose of making money off of it, and not really taking the time to care for the rabbit's particular needs.

Many people have had bad experiences purchasing pets from these local shops because most of the time rabbits die after they were brought home from the pet stores due to lack of adequate care. Pet stores also tend to take away the bunnies sometimes too early from their mother which is why they may be prone to many illnesses or has an unhealthy condition. Perhaps the only advantage of buying from pet stores is that it's near your house and you can get supplies any time with less hassle but as much as possible do not buy from pet shops.

Flea Markets

Another popular place to purchase a Jersey Wooly is from flea markets. Again these are not highly recommended because normally rabbits being sold in flea markets are of mixed rabbit breeds. So if you want a Jersey Wooly breed but you are not that familiar with it, chances are you'll end up buying another kind of rabbit breed (after all they all look the same). Another major disadvantage is that you don't know where these rabbits came from, you don't know their previous living condition, if they're healthy or not, and the breeder may not have taken care these rabbits properly. Yes, you can buy cheap rabbit breeds in flea markets that probably comes in all "shapes and sizes" but it's highly discouraged.

Rabbit Rescue Centers

If you want to buy a Jersey Wooly or any rabbit breed that could possibly be cheaper and you can also be assured of its quality, then go get them from rabbit rescue centers. This is a good place if you want to adopt a rabbit, perhaps the main advantage is that you can actually save a life if you decided to adopt a bunny. When it comes to quality, you can be assured that these bunnies are well taken care of, and you'll get to know the rabbit's health history since they are being kept by professionals. Sometimes rabbits from rescue centers are already spayed or neutered so you won't have a problem with that anymore. But it may not be a good idea to adopt a rabbit from a shelter if you want to breed rabbits or join a show.

Backyard Rabbit Breeders

One of the common and better places to purchase a rabbit is from backyard rabbit breeders. The reason for this is because these breeders are small time rabbit keepers, which means that they usually have only a couple of litter that is being sold. It also means that since they only take care of a couple of litters, you can be assured of its quality and health. You can also go back and ask the breeders questions in terms of the previous living condition, the food, the age, the breed, the health status etc. Be careful though because there are still some backyard breeders who only breeds rabbits because they want to get rid of their excess litter or just sell them.

Dedicated Rabbit Hobbyists

The last but definitely not the least is buying from dedicated rabbit enthusiasts. These people are generally the go – to place of any keepers who already have had some experience when it comes to buying rabbits. Dedicated hobbyists usually have larger rabbitries and they seriously know a lot about a particular breed that they're selling. These are the people who are reputable breeders because they don't just sell their pets to anyone; they also like to make sure that their bunnies will go to good homes. They care for their pets so much that they'll go the extra mile of making sure that you'll be ready to raise the bunnies that they bred. The only disadvantage is that the rabbits can be quite expensive, but you can be guaranteed of the quality, the health, and also the support system if you have further inquiries about the rabbit breed you purchase. It is worth investing in though because you won't have to worry about the health and   wellness of your pet in the long run, and also save you a lot of money.

License Requirements

If you are planning to acquire a Jersey Wooly rabbit as your pet, there are certain restrictions and regulations that you need to be aware of. Licensing requirements for rabbits varies in different countries, regions, and states. Here are some things you need to know regarding the acquirement of Jersey Wooly rabbits both in the U. S. and the U.K.

Before you bring home a new pet, it is always a good idea to determine whether there are any laws in your area which require you to register or license your pet. In many cases, a license or permit is only required for exotic or endangered animals, fortunately Jersey Wooly rabbits do not qualify. There are, however, some local regulations which may require you to license your rabbit. Some states may require rabbit owners to license their pets every year and the cost may be higher if the rabbit is not spayed or neutered.

If you plan to breed and sell rabbits, you may be subject to an entirely different set of regulations. Your business must be licensed unless you are only selling rabbits for meat or fiber. If you sell rabbits as pets, you do not need a license if your annual sales are under a certain revenue amount set by your state. As always, however, it is a good idea to research the regulations in your area before you do anything.

When it comes to owning rabbits in England, rabbit owners are not required to obtain a license or permit but if you plan to import a rabbit from outside the U.K. or export one outside the country, you will need to obtain an Animal Movement License (AML). This rule is in place because rabies has been eradicated from the U.K. and unregulated imports and exports of live animals could re-introduce the disease.

Traits of a Reputable Rabbit Breeder

Finding a reputable or responsible rabbit breeder is essential so that you'll know that you are getting a healthy pet. If you're having trouble determining if a particular breeder is the right one for you, then take note of the traits listed in this section so that you can easily spot a good breeder.

Trait #1: Reputable rabbit breeders know their material

- They know everything there is to know about the rabbit's breed – its pedigree, its family history, its health status, what the rabbit prefers in terms of food, housing, toys etc.
- They have an ARBA or BRC registrations and a license to make sure that they are keeping up with the standards.
- They know the exact measurements of the food, the frequency, the temperature and all the information about their rabbit's needs and their facilities.

Trait #2: Reputable rabbit breeders are willing to provide assistance to the potential buyers

- They will be willing to answer all your questions about raising or caring rabbits.
- They will be willing to give references from previous buyers.
- They will be willing to provide you the resources you might need for the rabbit you're going to purchase.

Trait #3: Reputable rabbit breeders will also ask about you or your reasons for keeping or caring a rabbit

- They will ask questions about your job, your financial capability, your house/living condition, other household pets (if any) and all the things that will satisfy the breeder's curiosity to know and make sure that his/her bunnies will be taken care of.

- This is a major sign that the breeder is responsible and not just after the money – that they actually care about their pets.

Trait #4: Reputable rabbit breeders obviously have good reputation

- You might want to buy from someone who is highly recommended from friends or other people because if they say nice things about him/her, chances are it's true.

- If many people recommend a particular breeder, why not see for yourself and see if this breeder checks out your criteria. Gather customer feedback from previous buyers if you can.

Trait #5: Reputable rabbit breeders gives a health guarantee or has a contract

- If the breeder has some kind of health guarantee or vaccination certificates then that means that he/she is reputable.

- If the breeder offers you a contract or you have a written agreement that he/she will be willing to re-acquire the pet from you if in case you won't be able to take care of it, that's a good sign that he/she is a responsible breeder.

Selecting a Healthy Rabbit Breed

Aside from finding a good breeder, it's also essential to select a healthy Jersey Wooly, you have to make sure that the rabbit you will choose is not just healthy but also someone who matches your personality or has a good behavior. Here are some tips on how to spot a healthy and happy rabbit.

- Take a few minutes to observe the litter as a whole, and watch how the rabbits interact with each other.

- The baby rabbits should be active and playful. They should be interacting with each other in a healthy way. Avoid any rabbits that appear to be lethargic and those that have difficulty moving because they could be sick.

- Interact with the rabbits by putting your hand into the cage or nesting box to give the baby rabbits time to sniff and explore you before you interact with them.

- Encourage them to play with a toy so you can see more of their personalities and determine if it matches yours.
- Try picking up the baby rabbit and hold him to see how he responds to human contact.

- Examine its body to make sure that there aren't any signs of health issues, injuries or inadequate living condition. Make sure the eyes, ears and snout have no discharge, and must be clear and clean. The body should be proportional and free of any health problems/injuries, and it should walk or hop normally without any sign of immobility.

Pros and Cons of Jersey Wooly Rabbits

Pros

- Jersey Woolies are cute and generally a low-maintenance pet.
- Grooming will not be a problem because their wools are easy to brush and they don't shed as much like other rabbit breeds
- These rabbits come in a variety of colors depending which allows you to choose the best option.
- Generally a good pet for smaller living spaces such as condos and apartments.
- Generally a friendly, docile, and playful pet to people as well as other household pets
- Jersey Woolies are easy to care for in terms of their diet, and husbandry.

Cons

- They may not want to be touch or handled all the time. Although they can be laid back lap bunnies, they may get stress if they are always being handled.

- May not be a good choice if you already have other huge household pets such as big dogs because they can get scared since rabbits are prey animals.
- Rabbits in general cannot be kept in their cages all the time; you need to give them enough space and time to explore around your house.
- Some Jersey Wooly rabbit breed may not be eligible for showing particularly for shows that are for pure bred rabbit species only.
- Jersey Woolies could keep you up at night because they are mostly active during nighttime.
- Cost for its maintenance/husbandry will definitely be additional expense.
- Can be a long-term commitment, Jersey Woolies live between 7 to 12 years or more.

Chapter Three: Housing and Maintenance Requirements

Jersey Wooly Rabbits don't take up too much space, and though buying or building a cage/hutch for them is recommended, they don't necessarily need it. But of course, you don't want them to escape or mess up your house, therefore your pet rabbit should be given adequate shelter for them to rest on, and also provide the adequate things needed so that they'll have live comfortably and be able to adjust to its new environment. Aside from all that, the main thing your rabbit needs in terms of its habitat is lots of love and affection from his owners or care takers, rabbits may not like to always be handled but even if that's the case it still bonds closely with family.

In this chapter you'll learn the basics about your rabbit's habitat requirements, the recommended cage accessories as well as the step by step process on how to build your own rabbit cage.

Housing Guidelines and Hutch Materials

Setting up a cage or housing for your Jersey Wooly is one of the fun parts of becoming rabbit keeper. You can get to decorate something cool, gather fun bunny materials for their hutch or try a do – it – yourself cage, whatever kind of enclosure you want to make, you have to keep in mind some guidelines to make sure that your Jersey wooly will be comfortable in his new home. Check out some tips below:

- Jersey wool rabbits are quite active animals which is why its cage should be large enough so that he can move around with ease. The cage itself should provide at least eight square feet of space for one or more rabbits.

- Purchase a rabbit cage that is two to three times the length of your rabbit so that even if he grows larger, he can still fit in it. For you to do this, you should take the time to at least have an estimate measurement of your rabbit's body.

- You also need to consider the materials from which your rabbit's cage will be made. Choose a cage that is easy to clean and durable; wooden cages may not be recommended because it absorbs moisture and harbor bacteria. Plastic cages and metal cages are highly recommended.

- You should avoid a cage with wire flooring because these can irritate your rabbit's feet. If ever you go with that option, just make sure to cover a portion of it with a square of carpet or a mat.

- You should provide an exercise pen in addition to a large cage. Your rabbit should get at least two to five hours a day in the exercise pen or if you are handy, you can connect the pen to his cage so he can come and go as he pleases. The exercise space should provide at least twenty five square feet of space.

- Food dishes for rabbits come in all shapes and sizes but you should choose a set that suits your Jersey wool's needs. Don't choose anything too small or too big and as mentioned earlier, stainless steel and ceramic bowls do not harbor bacteria and they are easy to clean.

- When it comes to your Jersey Wool rabbit's water bottle, you should choose a non-drip model because it will prevent you in constantly changing your pet's bedding.

- If you want to keep your rabbit's hay fresh, you should opt to purchase a hay feeder so that you can easily put it into your rabbit's cage. The best litter to use in a rabbit cage is fresh hay. You should opt to buy edible hay like meadow hay or timothy hay. You can also use a blanket made from some kind of natural fiber.

- When it comes to purchasing a litter pan, you need to buy something that is large enough for your rabbit to use and also deep enough to contain the litter, and also avoid contamination.

- You should also provide stimulating toys to prevent your pet from getting bored plus it also a form of exercise. It is ideal that you buy an assortment of toys at first and give your rabbit time to play with them so you can learn which type he prefers.

- You should also opt to buy chew toys to provide mental and physical stimulation.

- Keep in mind that your rabbit's cage should also have a hiding place or shelter with bedding. However, straw bedding, wood shavings, and pine beddings are not recommended for rabbit cages because it absorbs moisture which can lead to urine burn and it can also harbor bacteria. Make sure to consider the type of litter you want to use for your rabbit's bedding.

- Make sure to buy a fresh hay bedding, durable hay feeder, stainless water and food dishes, litter pan, and stimulating toys as well as other decorations for your rabbit's cage.

Do – It - Yourself Rabbit Cage

One of the most expensive items that people purchase for their rabbits is a rabbit cage. But if you want to save money and create something unique for your new companion, why not try a DIY Rabbit Cage? Here's a step by step process on how to build your own rabbit cage:

Step 1: Decide on a cage type and the kind of material you want to use. You can choose to make a wire cage but make sure that the flooring has a mat or a covering to prevent irritation of your rabbit's feet. Wire cage are much easy to clean, easier to move around, lasts longer and can even be cheaper to make than the traditional wood cages.

Step 2: Gather your Supplies. You can normally find wire available at your local feed or hardware store. Here is a list of supplies and equipment that you will need to build your rabbit cage:

- Hammer
- Wire Cutters
- J-Clip Pliers
- J-clips
- Wooden 2 x 4 (about 2 ft. long)
- Measure tape or yard stick

Step 3: Begin Building. Lay the side wire piece on the ground and grab the wooden 2 by 4 and your hammer. Next, using your hammer try to bend the wire around the corner of the wooden 2 by 4 to create the two 3 foot and 2 ½ foot sides.

Step 4: Finish the Sides. Once you have bent the wire start fastening the rectangle in place by clamping the J-clips on with your J-clip pliers. You should attach a clip about every 3 inches on the side.

Step 5: Attach the Bottom. The next thing to do is to attach the ½ inch by 1 inch mesh wire piece to the sides you just created with J-clips and pliers to make the bottom.

Step 6: Attach the Top. In the same way that you attached the bottom attach the 1 inch by 2 inch mesh wire piece to form the top of the cage.

Step 7: Build the Door. Next step is to cut an opening of about 1 foot square on the wide side of the wire using your pair of wire clippers. Be sure to leave approximately ½ inch stubs on the cut wire. And then do your best to bend the wire stubs back with the clippers so that the edges are smooth and then attach the door wire piece.

Step 8: Decide on a Cage Location. Pick a spot on your rabbit's cage where you would like hay feeder to hang. Keep in mind that the hay rack should not hang on the door of the cage or next to your rabbit's water bottle.

Step 9: Gather your materials (again). You will need to get out your pair of gloves and wire clippers to cutout the wire for the hay feeder. The wire cutting should be around six inches wide and eight inches long.

Step 10: Start Constructing. Take the piece of wire and bend its two opposite sides into a rectangular U shape. Try to make one side slightly higher than the other and be sure to leave an opening at the top and on the sides.

Step 11: Pay attention to details. Be sure to clip off any sharp edges on your hay rack to ensure the safety of your rabbit because it might rub its chin against the structure and get injured.

Step 12: Attach the rack or hay feeder. Now it is time to attach the new hay rack to your rabbit's cage. Attach the hay rack to one of the sides of your rabbit's cage using a leash clip. Be sure that the hay rack is secure in its new location.

Step 13: Collect the dust. If you have your rabbit's cage is indoors, then it is recommended that you place a piece of plastic under the hay rack to catch any dust that might fall through.

Chapter Four: Feeding Your Jersey Wooly Rabbits

When it comes to feeding rabbits, most people assume that these cute bunnies only eat carrots! For those of you who are newbies, that's not entirely true. Yes they do eat carrots but they also need to be provided with nutritious food from various food sources so that they can have a balance diet and be strong against diseases. In this section, you'll learn the majority of your pet's nutritional needs as well as feeding tips and foods that are good and harmful for your pet rabbit.

Rabbit Nutrition

All animals need to have a balanced diet which is why it is important to pay attention to the contents of your rabbit's food. When it comes to your rabbit's nutrition, you need to make sure that he/she is getting enough protein, fiber and fat percentages.

Protein

Protein plays a major role in helping your rabbits grow and stay in good health especially if you are breeding rabbits. Many breeders recommend feeding your breeding does (or pregnant female rabbits) a higher protein feed to help with milk production. You can opt to feed your Jersey Wooly rabbit/s around 15% - 18% of protein feed.

Fiber

You also want to make sure that your Jersey Wooly gets enough fiber content in its food. Fiber is important in helping your rabbit digest their food and keep their gut moving. You can incorporate about 18% fiber grain in your rabbit's diet. You can also supplement a lower fiber feed with some grass hay. Hay is also a good source of fiber for rabbits.

Fats

It is ideal to pay attention to the amount of fat that your rabbit food contains. The grain or commercial pellet that is ideal for your Jersey Wooly is about 2.5% fats. If your rabbit feed contains too much fat, it might cause trouble down the road because there is a good chance that your pet will get overweight. And if your breeding does get too fat, their chance of producing large litters of kits will be greatly reduced. Enough fat is essential though because it is a key ingredient in your rabbit's diet; it can help your rabbits grow a nice fur coat.

Safe and Toxic Foods

When feeding your Jersey Wooly rabbit, make sure you don't go overboard with the portions and you should also introduce new foods slowly. On the other hand, never ever feed your rabbit anything unless you are really sure that it is safe.

Here is a list of foods that are safe for your Jersey Wooly rabbits:

- Snow Peas
- Melons
- Star Fruit
- Edible flowers
- Celery
- Cherries
- Pear
- Peach
- Apricot
- Currants
- Nectarines
- Brussel sprouts
- Cabbage (any type)
- Bell peppers

- Apple
- Carrots
- Broccoli
- Plum
- Mango
- Summer squash
- Zucchini
- Kiwi
- Papaya
- Banana
- Berries
- Pineapple
- Wheat grass

Here are some foods that are toxic for your Jersey Wooly rabbit and should be avoided:

- Candy
- Gum
- Coffee
- Citrus peels
- Corn
- Bread
- Chocolate
- Beets
- Seeds
- Fresh peas
- Grains
- Avocado
- Nuts
- Onions
- Green beans
- Legumes Potatoes
- Rice
- Rhubarb

FAQs about Feeding Rabbits

When should I feed my rabbit?

Most breeders recommend feeding rabbits at night because they are mostly active at night, and they'll also eat their food more during nighttime. Rabbits might also snub the food if the grains become moist during the day especially if it is summertime. If you can't feed them at night for some reason, you can also opt to feed them early in the morning because they are also active at this time.

Should I feed my rabbit more than once?

If you feed your rabbit multiple times in a day, it may cause them to become overweight in the long run. Feeding them more than once or more than the needed amount is not good for their health, once a day feeding at night or early morning is appropriate.

How will my rabbit drink?

Water is important so that your pet will not be dehydrated especially during the warm season. Make sure that your rabbit has access to fresh water supply all the time by using an automatic watering system or using some kind of water dripper. Some keepers still use water bowls/dishes as well. The important thing is that your rabbit can access it anytime he/she wants to drink.

What are the highly recommended food brands for rabbits?

You can purchase from brands like Petrus, Purina, Manna Pro, Sherwood Forest Natural Rabbit Food and the likes.

What is the ratio or amount of food for my young and adult Jersey Wooly?

Usually baby Jersey woolies only consume their mother's milk with small portions of alfalfa hay or baby pellets until about 12 weeks. After 3 months you can slowly introduce veggies and other types of pellets or hays to see what your rabbit prefers. After about 7 months you can then feed them ½ cup of grass hay, oat hay or other types but make sure to decrease the pellet food. You can also start increasing the vegetables of one cup per six pounds of your rabbit's body weight. After 1 year, you can then introduce fruits and some treats in small quantities. Once it reaches maturity around 2 years and beyond, then you can provide them with an unlimited access to hays, veggies, fruits and some treats. Of course this will still depend on your Jersey wooly's current weight, make sure to go to the vet regarding the exact portion of food that you should give to your Jersey Wooly because it highly depends on the age and current body weight of your pet.

Should I just feed my rabbit a commercial pellet food or fresh diet or both?

It actually depends upon you, some breeders only feed commercial pellet food for their rabbits since it is already packed with essential nutrients, vitamins and minerals plus it is easy to buy and prepare. Some breeders choose to only feed their rabbits with fresh veggies and fruits as well as some grains while some people do both. It's better to give your pet rabbit a few options, and see what it prefers. You can also take note the effects of such diets so that you'll know what works best for your Jersey Wooly.

Feeding Tips and Tricks

Here are some tips and tricks that could help you in feeding your rabbits:

- Feed your rabbits some type of hay on a frequent basis
- The most effective rabbit food is a nice pellet based feed with veggies and fruits from time to time
- Don't over-feed your does or you might not get any bunnies
- Evaluate the contents of a rabbit feed bag before making a purchase
- Growing bunnies will generally stay healthiest when they are free fed

- If your rabbit isn't eating its pellets try feeding him or her some green grass.
- Sometimes if a rabbit doesn't eat much of its food, it could be a sign that something is wrong with it or its water supply.
- Don't feed your rabbit candy or sweets. If you want to feed them treats make sure that it is a rabbit safe treats.
- In the summer rabbits will generally consume less food.
- If you show your rabbits, you can limit their daily intake of vegetables.
- If you consistently change out your rabbits' diet, be sure to keep a notebook of the changes that you have made so that if something goes wrong you can easily detect if it is caused by the food or not.
- When buying rabbits from a breeder, be sure to ask them the brand of food they gave to your rabbit so that there will be consistency

Chapter Five: Rabbit Husbandry

Husbandry is very important to maintain your Jersey Wooly's health and condition. Providing a nice housing or enclosure as well as feeding it properly with nutritious foods will go a long way but you also have to make sure that their emotional needs are taken care of so that they will have lower chances of getting ill or becoming too shy or overly aggressive. In this chapter you'll learn how to properly handle, carry, train and tame your cute Jersey Wooly. You'll also get to learn on how to groom them to maintain their coat and skin.

Handling and Carrying Rabbits

Jersey woolies don't particularly like to be handled for long periods of time. Sure they are very cuddly looking and it seems like they are really sweet creatures but most rabbits hate to be constantly touch or handled too much especially with strangers. In this section you'll learn how to handle and carry rabbits.

How to Remove a Rabbit from its Cage

Rabbits usually struggle if they are being removed from their cages, follow these tips so you can carefully and properly handle them so that they won't be stressed out whenever you are cleaning their cage.

- Your palms should be place in your pet's abdomen; once you do that's when you lift them up.
- If your pet struggle or isn't comfortable you can use your other hand to support the shoulders and/or grip its skin.
- Once you have lifted it out of the cage, you should provide support to its legs using your hand or lean it over your body.

How to Carry a Rabbit

There are many ways for you to carry your rabbit; in this section we'll provide you with different methods on how you can carry your pet Jersey Wooly. Sometimes one method may not work or your pet may not be that comfortable so make sure to test if this is the kind of handling your Jersey Wooly will prefer.

Method #1:

- Hold your pet's ears and its shoulders in your right hand while placing its feet on your left arm.
- Support your rabbit's rear with your left hand
- Finally tuck your Jersey wooly's head under your left elbow.

Method #2:

- Place your pet's feet on your chest or tummy, then support its rear behind using your left hand
- Finally, keep a slightly tight grip on your rabbit with your right hand so that it won't try to escape or jump

Method #3:

- Hold your pet's ears and its shoulders in your right hand while placing its feet on your left arm.
- Lift up its behind with your left hand and make sure that its head is facing towards you

Grooming and Litter Training Your Rabbit

When it comes to grooming, you'll have no problem maintaining your Jersey Wooly's fur because even if its coat is dense, it is very easy to brush. In fact, you don't really need to brush it daily, you can however brush it once or twice a week to maintain its beautiful fur and avoid any debris on its coat. You will get a feel for how often to brush your rabbit as you see how much he sheds on a regular basis.

When it comes to litter training, rabbits are naturally fairly clean animals and they tend to choose one or two places in their cage to urinate and defecate. This makes your job very easy. All you have to do is watch your rabbit for a few days to determine where he tends to relieve himself and then simply place a litter pan in that area. Some rabbits choose a single location and others choose two or more. Usually though, it is located in the corners of cage.

After discovering where your rabbit likes to relieve himself, you need to determine which type of litter you want to use. Avoid cat litters because they are often dusty or scented. The best litter to use is something organic made from alfalfa or oat hay, even paper. You can also simply use fresh hay as your litter. You want to avoid wood shavings, sawdust, and shredded newspaper or cardboard because they can absorb moisture as well as something made out of cedar or pine because it can be harmful for your pet.

Grooming Guidelines

- Most rabbits hate getting wet and that includes your Jersey Wooly! Never ever give your rabbit a full soaking bath even if for some reason they became really dirty or smelly because this could actually be extremely stressful for your pet. It takes a rabbit a very long time to dry especially for furry coated Jersey Woolies, which is why bathing could actually put your rabbit at risk for pneumonia. You are better off spot-cleaning his coat as needed with a damp cloth.

- The only time you may need to bathe your rabbit is if he/she has a high fever or if your vet recommends a cooling bath to bring down your rabbit's body temperature.

- When it comes to trimming your rabbit's nails you need to be very careful because a rabbit's nails contain a quick which is pinkish part at the base of the nail that contains the blood vessel and nerves for that nail. When trimming your rabbit's nails, it is best to just trim off the sharp tip.

- If you accidentally clip your rabbit's nails too short, you could injure them and it could lead to profuse bleeding. Make sure to always keep some styptic powder, flour or some medication to stop the bleeding in case you cut the nail too short.

- In terms of cleaning your Jersey Wooly's ears, he may not be prone to ear infections because it has erect ears which means that if your rabbit's ears get wet, they could harbor bacteria growth which could lead to an infection. Rabbits with erect ears have a lower risk for infection because their ears are open and get plenty of air flow.

- In order to clean your Jersey Wooly's ears, just dip a cotton ball in a mild antiseptic solution and squeeze out any excess liquid. Use the cotton ball to wipe any ear wax or debris from your rabbit's ears then let it dry.

- When it comes to your rabbit's teeth, you should make sure that it is checked by a veterinarian at least twice a year so that he can trim your rabbit's teeth if necessary

Chapter Six: Breeding Your Jersey Wooly Rabbit

If you want to become a reputable rabbit breeder or you simply have grown fond of taking care of more than one rabbit, then this chapter is for you! Rabbit breeding is one of the most significant factors that will help determine the long term success of your rabbitry. As we all know rabbits can be excellent breeders, however many rabbit raisers struggle with getting their rabbits to breed for several different reasons.

In this chapter you'll learn some basic things about breeding your Jersey Wooly and the things you need to consider so that you can be make sure that you are committed if you decided to go down this 'rabbit hole.'

Reasons to Breed Rabbits

As with anything else, before you do something, you should always start with your "why." Yes, even in breeding rabbits! The reason for this is for you to really know if this is an endeavor you want to do, and will enjoy doing despite of all the responsibilities you need to take. So to start with, here is a short list of reasons why people breed rabbits in the first place, see if this is one of the reasons why you want to become a legit rabbit breeder:

- The process of raising and caring for baby bunnies can be a fun and interesting learning experience
- Rabbit breeding can be a profitable business
- Many rabbit shows judge rabbits at market age, so exhibitors need to have approximately 10 week old bunnies to be eligible to show
- Rabbit meat is proven to be one of the healthiest meats available for consumption (although this may not be a good reason).
- Bunny rabbits make excellent photography subjects

- Around Easter each year there is a high demand for pet rabbits

Things to Consider Before Breeding

Now that you have determined your personal reason why you want to become a rabbit breeder, the next step is to consider the things you need to handle before you even began breeding. Here's a list of things you should take note before beginning your breeding endeavor:

- Successfully raising up bunny rabbits will require a dedication of time and labor
- Rabbit rescue centers are filled with unwanted rabbits
- Many first time rabbit raisers find it difficult to get rid of excess rabbits
- Bunnies will grow up quickly and require more space (so be prepared)
- You will need to purchase or make a nest box for each doe that you breed
- No matter what you do, bunnies will occasionally die (this is the reason that rabbits are made to have such large litters)
- In case of a crisis, you will need to have enough knowledge to save your bunnies.

FAQS about Rabbit Breeding

Now that you have taken into consideration the risks and responsibilities of becoming a rabbit breeder, it's now time to get into the basics of breeding these cute bunch.

Is there a rabbit breeding season or cycle?

Most animals have a breeding season; their fertility and willingness to breed is often determined by this cycle. The good news is that rabbits including the Jersey Wooly don't tend to have a breeding cycle. Some rabbit raisers have claimed that rabbits tend to have a 3 to 4 day cycle each month where their chance of getting pregnant is minimal. As long as you have a healthy doe and an eager buck, cycles or breeding seasons don't really matter. In fact, some female rabbits living in the wild will get pregnant up to eight times a year.

When should I breed my rabbits?

If your purpose for raising rabbits is to produce home grown meat for your family or simply to raise rabbits for pets, then for the most part you will have the luxury of deciding when you want to breed your rabbits, although majority of rabbit breeders breed at certain times of the year for other reasons.

If you plan on showing rabbits at meat pen shows then you will be required to breed your rabbits almost on an exact day in order to produce kits with the right age for the show but if your goal is to raise rabbits for profits, it is important to take into account your target market when deciding when to breed. Some markets will only accept bunnies at certain times of the year while others will demand bunnies year round.

When is the ideal season to breed my Jersey Wooly rabbits?

The ideal seasons to breed your pet rabbits are spring, fall and winter. If you live in a cooler climate such as in the northern United States, then summer can be a great option. Rabbits in general thrive best in mild climates which is one of the reasons why western states like California have become such a popular place to raise rabbits. Rabbits on the other hand tend to prefer cold climates over hot climates.

How Often Should I breed?

In order to keep your rabbits in good breeding health you need to breed your rabbits at least three times a year. However, if you fail to breed your rabbits enough, your does can build up internal fat in their uterus, which will reduce their chance of getting pregnant or simply reduce their average litter size in general. Although many commercial breeders will breed their does six times a year, for the general rabbit raiser it is best to breed your does between 3 and 4 times a year.

How long is a rabbit's gestation cycle?

Jersey Wooly rabbits' gestation cycle take approximately 30 days from breeding to kindling. In general though, the rabbit pregnancy cycle usually last between 28 and 32 days.

What is the average litter size for Jersey Wooly?

The average litter for Jersey Wooly is 3 – 4 bunnies sometimes more.

Do – It – Yourself Nesting Box

Most rabbit breeders would agree on the fact that nest boxes are essential kindling supplies that any rabbit raiser should obtain if they plan on breeding their does. Nest boxes help keep your new born bunnies safe and warm. In addition to that it also gives your doe a sense of security. If you have multiple does it can get expensive to have to buy all your nest boxes so why not try to build it yourself? Here's a step by step process on how to build a DIY nesting box.

Step 1: Decide on a model. There are several different nest box models that you can choose to build such as a wooden nest boxes, wood and wire nest boxes and all metal nest boxes. There are also several different types of each of these models that come in all different sizes and dimensions. Some rabbit breeders prefer different models for different reasons, so you are free to choose which model you like best. I personally prefer using the Wooden Enclosed Nest Box.

Step 2: Buy the materials you need. The first step to constructing wooden enclosed nest boxes is to purchase several sheets of plywood which will be used to build the nest box frame. One of the best things about wooden nest boxes is the fact that they are cheap and easy to make.

Step 3: Cut the plywood. Cut the wood in the following dimensions:

- 2 Sides: 19 in. wide by 13 in. tall
- Front: 14 in. wide by 13 in. tall
- Back: 13 in. wide by 12.5 in. tall
- Bottom: 19 in. long by 13 in. wide
- Top: 19.5 in. long by 14 in. wide

Step 4: Cutout an opening: You will need cutout a section of the board so that your rabbit can access the nest box. You can draw a line down the middle of the width of the board and then divide the board into four quadrants. And then cut out either the upper left or right quadrant of the board.

Step 5: Nailing time! Use small nails to nail the bottom board to the front board (make sure the cut-out in the board is facing the top) and then go around and nail the other boards (except the top) in place. The back board should be on top of the bottom board so that the height is even with the sides.

Step 6: Almost done! You should now have your whole nest box created except for the top. Next set up the top board to rest on top of the other boards and make sure that it is aligned properly. Get a screw driver and drill four holes in the sides of the top board. Ideally, the holes in the top board should be a bit larger than the screws so that you can lift the board off the top of the screws with a little effort.

Step 7: The finishing touches. Finish drilling the screws into the sides of the board. You want the screws to stay in place in the sides of the boards. Don't expand the holes like what you did to the top board.

Chapter Seven: Showing Your Jersey Wooly Rabbit

The Jersey Wooly is not a pure bred rabbit but it can still be eligible for some shows in various organizations and competitions. In order to show your Jersey Wooly rabbit, however, you have to make sure that he meets the requirements for the breed standard and you need to learn the basics about showing rabbits. In this chapter you will learn more about the specific standard for the Jersey Wooly breed and receive some tips for entering your rabbit in a show. Have fun!

Jersey Wooly Breed Standard

Jersey Wooly Schedule of Points:

- General Type – 58
- Body – 30
- Head – 16
- Ears – 10
- Eyes – 2
- Feet and Legs – 0
- Wool – 27
- Texture – 14
- Density – 8
- Length – 5
- Color – 10
- Condition – 5

TOTAL POINTS - 100

Showmanship

If you decide to show your rabbit, you must become a member of either the ARBA (if you are in U.S) or the BRC (if you're based in England) organization. Once you have become a member you will be able to register your rabbit under your name and enter him in shows. It can sometimes take a little while to complete this process so stay up to date with shows in your area so you can enter your rabbit as soon as your registration is completed.

Showmanship Guidelines

- Start by reading the rules and regulations for that specific show. In most cases, registering your rabbit for a show is fairly easy but you want to make sure you don't overlook anything that might get you disqualified.

- Make sure you adhere to the deadlines for registration and have all of the information you are likely to need handy.

- Make sure to provide your name and address, the breed of your rabbit, its color and age, and the sex of your rabbit. Sometimes they will also ask whether you bred or transferred the rabbit or whether you are a new exhibitor

- Prior to the day of show, make sure that you know how to get there and you have a copy of the schedule so that you know exactly when your rabbit is to be shown. In the days leading up to the show you should put together a kit of items that may come in handy on show day such as your rabbit's registration information, food and water, nail clippers, hydrogen peroxide (for cleaning injuries and spots on white coats), slicker brush and other grooming supplies, business cards, contact information, paper towels and wet wipes, scrap carpet square (for last minute grooming), extra clothes, food, and water for yourself.

- Plan to arrive at the venue at least an hour prior to judging, and then proceed to your assigned pen. Prepare your rabbit and check everything (again). Try observing people and other rabbits so that you'll gain an insight as to how things work during showing day.

- When it comes time for judging, all you can really do is wait and let the judges do their duties. Your rabbit must remain in his pen for the duration of the judging. If you rabbit wins anything, a prize card will be placed on his pen. When the judging is over, you can take your prize cards to the secretary and collect your prize money.

- After the show, you can stick around to keep learning. Take advantage of this opportunity to connect with other rabbit owners – you never know what you might learn or how a new connection could benefit you.

Chapter Eight: Health Problems: Symptoms, Causes and Treatments

While you may not be able to prevent your Jersey Wooly rabbit from getting sick in certain situations, you can be responsible in educating yourself about the diseases that could affect your pet rabbit. The more you know about these potential health problems, the better you will be able to identify them and to seek immediate veterinary care when needed.

In this chapter you will be provided with some of the most common health problems affecting rabbits. You as the potential keeper should also learn how to strengthen your bunny's resistance to common illnesses by having regular checkup with their vets so we've also included some guidelines on how you find a good rabbit savvy vet to look after your pet.

Bacterial Diseases

Sniffles Disease

- Sniffles disease is another common bacterial infection in rabbits. When caught early, sniffles can be treated, but it can quickly become chronic or even fatal.
- This disease is a respiratory infection caused by the bacteria *Pasteurella multocida* and it is highly infectious. There are several different strains of the bacteria which can affect the rabbit's eyes, ears and various other organs.
- The signs of sniffles can vary depending on the strain and the progression of the disease but generally include a watery nasal discharge, sneezing, and a loud snuffling or snoring sound.

- This disease can also travel to the eyes, causing conjunctivitis, and to the ears, causing head shaking, head tilt, disorientation, and a loss of balance. It is also possible for this disease to affect the rabbit's reproductive tract and it may also result in the formation of pus-filled sores.
- This disease is so contagious and dangerous, prevention through strict sanitation and quarantine procedures is a must.
- The most common treatment for sniffles disease is a fifteen to thirty day course of antibiotics and supplementary probiotics.

Urine Scald

- Usually occurs when urine soaks into the rabbit's fur and causes severe inflammation and hair loss.
- The common cause is unsanitary conditions, when strict sanitation practices are not followed, the cage can harbor bacteria.
- If you do not clean your rabbit's cage often enough or if you fail to keep his litter box fresh, your rabbit may be forced to sit in his own urine which can lead to this painful condition.
- This problem can also develop from a rabbit's inability to control his bladder due to some

underlying medical condition or a physical inability to assume the right stance for urination.

- The most common sign of urine scald in rabbits is inflammation and redness around its private area.
- The best treatment for this is to apply a soothing ointment. You should also take steps to improve the sanitation in your rabbit's cage to prevent a recurrence of the problem. Make sure to keep your rabbit's cage clean and dry at all times.

Abscesses

- An abscess is a pocket of fluid and pus generally cause by a bacterial infection. These are fairly common in domestic rabbits and they can form anywhere on the rabbit's body.
- The cause of an abscess could be any number of things including a bite, a cut, or some other kind of wound.
- It may also be caused by foreign bodies becoming embedded in the rabbit's skin or mouth. They can also be the result of wounds in the mouth caused by dental disease.
- A mouth abscess can be very painful for your Jersey Wooly rabbit and it may cause him to stop eating.

- Another sign is that he may also drool and drop bits of food when he does eat. Abscesses on the skin usually appear as hard lumps.
- The best treatment for an abscess is to drain the fluid and pus which is usually performed under general anesthesia.
- The wound must be kept clean and the rabbit should take antibiotics to prevent infection.
- Painkillers may also be prescribed by your veterinarian.

Pneumonia

- Pneumonia is fairly common in domestic rabbits and it is generally caused by bacterial or sometimes viral infection which leads to inflammation in the lungs.
- Pneumonia can result from four different types of infections. It is also possible for environmental factors such as chemicals, smoke, or dental disease to cause inflammation which leads to pneumonia.
- The type of infection will determine the severity of the disease as well as the proper course of treatment. Rabbits suffering from fever, anorexia, weight loss, or lethargy may require fluid and electrolyte therapy. During treatment, your rabbit's movement should be restricted.

- Your vet may also prescribe antiviral, antimicrobial, antifungal, or antibiotic medications depending on the type of infection causing your rabbit's pneumonia.

Viral Diseases

Viral Hemorrhagic Disease (RVHD)

- Viral Hemorrhagic Disease is a viral disease that is highly infectious and can also affect domesticated rabbits like the Jersey Wooly.
- This disease causes severe fever accompanied by inflammation of the intestines, damage to the lymph nodes, and even liver damage. It may be detected through medical check – up by your vet or through blood tests and other medical examination.
- If left untreated, the Viral Hemorrhagic Disease can lead to a condition affecting the blood which prevents it from coagulating.
- It can also lead to massive ruptures of blood vessels in various organs.
- Most rabbits affected by this virus do not show any outward signs and many die within 24 hours of the onset of fever.
- Some of the symptoms that your rabbit may show include difficulty breathing, weight loss, lethargy,

paralysis, and convulsions. This disease is spread through direct contact or through contact with contaminated food, water or bedding.

- To prevent the spread of virus, it is highly recommended that you always keep your rabbit's cage clean and sanitize.
- There is no effective treatment for Viral Hemorrhagic Disease and it is usually fatal.

Infectious Myxomatosis

- This is a viral infection known to affect rabbits and it is caused by a virus in the poxvirus family. This disease is generally transmitted through insects and, in many cases, it is fatal.
- Myxomatosis is spread through blood-sucking insects like mosquitos, ticks, and lice, though direct transmission is possible.
- Clinical signs may vary depending on the strain but may include lethargy, loss of appetite, fever, swelling around the eyes, and swelling or drooping of the ears.
- Unfortunately, there is no effective treatment for myxomatosis and it is usually fatal. The best way to prevent this disease from occurring is to protect your rabbit against external parasites.

- If your rabbit does catch the disease, you need to
  employ careful sanitation practices to prevent the
  spread of this virus.
- This virus is extremely resistant to inactivation, and
  most rabbits exposed to myxomatosis must be
  quarantined for fourteen days to confirm infection.

Fungal Diseases and External Parasitic Conditions

Mange Mites

- Mange mites represent one of the most common skin
  problems in domestic rabbits. Such mites are invisible
  to the naked eye and can be easily spread through
  contaminated hay and bedding.
- The cause of mange mite infestations is still unknown,
  but it is likely that some rabbits carry the mites
  unknowingly and problems only develop when the
  rabbit is weakened by stress, illness, or injury. Mange
  mites feed on keratin which leads to poor coat
  condition and quality.
- The most common sign of mange mites in rabbits is
  patches of dandruff appearing on the coat, usually at
  the base of the tail and the nape of the neck. In cases

of severe infection, the patch may actually look like it
is moving because it is so heavily covered in mites.

- Treatment for mange mites generally involves
  ivermectin injection as well as a thorough cleaning
  and disinfecting of the rabbit's habitat.

- Regular grooming will also help prevent reinfection
  by removing dead hairs that mites could eat.

Ringworm

- Ringworm is not a disease caused by a worm or any
  other parasite – it is a fungal infection common in
  rabbits and other small mammals.

- There are several different types of fungus which can
  cause ringworm in rabbits and it can actually be
  transmitted to humans as well. In many cases, a rabbit
  is infected with the fungus by another rabbit or by
  another household pet could be a carrier but maybe
  asymptomatic.

- Poor sanitation, stress, high humidity, overcrowding,
  and malnutrition can all increase your rabbit's risk for
  acquiring this infection.

- The first sign of ringworm in most cases is the
  development of patchy areas of hair loss that are dry
  and flaky.

- Rabbits generally development lesions on their head, legs and feet first which can then spread to other parts of the body.
- Most rabbits recover from ringworm without treatment if sanitation in their cage improves.
- Treatment with anti-fungal medications may be necessary; during treatment you also need to thoroughly clean and disinfect everything in the cage to prevent reinfection.

E. Cuniculi

- This disease is caused by a small protozoan parasite called Encephalitozoon Cuniculi that can be absorbed into the rabbit's body through the intestines
- It generally causes lesions on the kidneys, brain, and other organs. This parasite can even be passed down from mother to baby or through direct contact with an infected rabbit.
- The most common symptoms of E. Cuniculi include loss of balance, head tilt, tremors, convulsions, blindness, partial paralysis, and coma or death.
- The treatment most commonly prescribed for this disease is Panacur, which can be administered in a 28 day course to destroy the parasite, through some veterinarians recommend re-treatment four times a

year to prevent reinfection. It is important to note, however, that this treatment is only effective in killing the parasite before symptoms appear.

Tips in Finding a Savvy Rabbit Veterinarian

- Ask for referral from your friends who are also rabbit keepers. Chances are they know a vet who are rabbit experts

- You can look at various rabbit organizations for a list of recommended rabbit vets. These vets applied to be on the recommended list and were approved by these organizations which mean that they somehow pass the standards.

- You can check other sources online to find a savvy vet or someone who is really knowledgeable. You can always go to their clinic and interview them to see if you prefer them.

- You have to make sure that the rabbit vet you prefer are aware of the importance of hospitalizing rabbits. You need to make sure that just in case your rabbit will need hospitalization, it will be placed in a separate kennel area away from other animals because the sounds of dogs, cats or other animals can be very stressful for rabbits since they are prey animals and may hinder recovery.

- You might also want to ask a vet if he/she recently completed further study such as a Continuing Professional Development (CPD) course. You may want a vet who likes to attend rabbit lectures, workshops and the likes because that's a good sign that he/she are always seeking to improve him/herself regarding rabbits.

- Vets should also recommend vaccinations for your rabbits. Such vaccinations should be to fight off diseases like RVHD and Myxomatosis. It's the basic vaccine all domesticated rabbits should get, if your vet doesn't recommend any vaccine at all, you're best moving on.

Chapter Nine: Marketing Your Rabbits

For those who are interested in becoming a legit and reputable rabbit raiser, especially for those who like to earn some revenue through this rabbit breeding practice then this chapter is for you! You can either make profit by selling your rabbits or selling rabbit meats, but before you do, you need to establish yourself first as someone who is a responsible breeder so that you'll attract more customers or even become a rabbit meat supplier. Learn how you can turn these rabbits into profits! Check out our tips and guidelines on how you can properly market and sell your rabbit breeds, and make money while enjoying this wonderful raising hobby.

Common Problem in Marketing or Selling Rabbits

Below are the most common problems when it comes to marketing or selling rabbits as well as some troubles during production or the breeding process. If you are aware of these instances, you'll be able to prevent it from happening or you'll be able to handle the situation.

- Breeding rabbits are often crowded into hutches due to herd overpopulation which may result in spread of illnesses or become stressful for the rabbits.
- Many times herd overpopulation leads to another problem such as poor herd management.
- Breeders are usually falling behind on management tasks
- Sometimes the owners get overwhelmed and decide to quit raising rabbits altogether
- Show animals tend to not perform as well as the keeper would have hoped
- Herd illnesses may be more prevalent due to lack of disease control and cleanliness
- Some owners may begin to increase their stock prices in order to help cover the cost of the additional feed they are buying

Qualities of a Reputable Rabbitry

Here are some things to keep in mind to make sure that the rabbits you are selling are of great quality and your customers will put in a good word for your rabbit business.

- The place or facility should be clean and well organized
- The rabbits should have hutches of their own to reside in and to avoid being crowded
- The owner should always keep everything on tract, and has rabbitry records for all the bunnies.
- Rabbitry management chores should be done in a time efficient manner so that everything is in place.
- If they participate in showing the breeders will often have good success with their rabbits on the judging table.
- Most importantly the owners should have a fun and enjoyable rabbit raising experience.

How to Earn to Money Off of Rabbits

In this section, we'll give you an idea on where you can sell your rabbit or how you can earn money if you choose to become a breeder.

Rabbit Meat Market

The most popular outlet to sell excess rabbits is the rabbit meat market. If people didn't consume rabbit meat there probably wouldn't even be half of the interest in rabbit raising that there is today. Even if you choose not to consume rabbit meat yourself you most likely will at least help supply this market with meat.

If you breed rabbits you will either be doing one of the following three things; eating rabbit yourself, selling rabbits for meat, and selling breeding stock that produce meat for either another rabbit raiser or market. Of course, if you plan on simply raising up a small pet rabbit breed you may be an exemption from these rules.

There are actually three different ways that you can earn and save money if you choose to sell your rabbit breeds as a rabbit meat. You can sell live rabbit (for its meat); sell rabbit meat in packages or eat the rabbit meat (much like a chicken or pork raiser).

Selling Live Rabbit

The easiest way to cover rabbitry expenses is to sell live rabbit meat to local markets or people who like to purchase or eat rabbit meat. You can sell your excess breeds to meat processors, so that you don't have to deal with all the work involved with slaughtering rabbits.

Selling Rabbit Meat Packages

If you are desperate to get rid of rabbits the best option for you might be to slaughter and process the rabbits yourself, and then sell the meat. But of course, you have to make sure that you can handle the killing part otherwise you might do it wrong. Perhaps it's better to get a mentor or a breeder who have done this before so you can have some help with this process.

Eating the Rabbit Meat

If you don't have a problem with processing or eating your own rabbits, then this might be a better option for you. Although you usually won't make any money off of this method, if you do things right you may just be able to save some money off your weekly grocery bill by eating home grown rabbit meat.

Laboratory Market (for animal experimentation)

Once you have become an established rabbit breeder with a good reputation and/or large herd you might just be able to sell some of your excess stock to a laboratory market. One of the main purposes of the rabbit laboratory market is to test out skin products that are made for humans because rabbits and humans have similarities when it comes to their skin reactions. Although the laboratory market turns down many rabbit breeders due to the fact that they worry about the fate of their beloved rabbits, nowadays though, there are strict regulations in place for animal experimentation.

Pet Market

Over the last two decades the rabbit pet market has grown big time, so if you are raiser who breeds many small to medium size rabbit breeds you may just be in a great position to take advantage of this growing market.

Breeding Stock Market

Most of the time the selling of rabbit breeding stock is what gives you the potential to make a good profit off of your rabbit breed or herd. The key to earning money off of breeding stock animals is to focus on quality not quantity because most buyers want to purchase the best breed that their money can buy not just as many as they can buy. Quality over quantity!

Evaluating Breeding Stock

One of the most important parts of raising rabbits is being able to evaluate breeding stock. Your ability to distinguish the good from the bad is very important in determining the long term success of your rabbitry. You need to develop an ability to be able to pick out the best rabbits from a litter, and decide if you will either keep them or sell them to others. Many reputable rabbit breeders know that when it comes to selling rabbits and evaluating stocks, it takes a ton of practice and patience.

In the next section, you'll learn about the qualities for a great breeding stock as well as the importance of maintaining healthy does and bucks.

Qualities of a Great Breeding Stock Rabbit

- The rabbits should remain healthy and would only require very little treatment
- The rabbits from a great breeding stock usually grows faster than the rest of the bunnies born in the litter
- The rabbit breeds stays in good condition during harsh weather (either during humid days or winter)
- Rabbits that willingly breeds
- Rabbits that produces large litters of healthy offspring
- The rabbit has a good body type

Importance of a Good Body Type among Rabbit Stocks

Regardless of whether you are breeding for meat, as household pets, show animals or for wool quality (for Jersey Woolies or similar rabbit species), it is important to keep nice big healthy rabbits. Ideally, you want to breed rabbit stock that has broad shoulders, a good loin, and good hindquarters.

If you are raising one of the more fancy breeds of rabbits you should put more emphasis on markings and fur. These rabbits that exhibit these traits are bound to be your best producers due to the fact that they tend to carry the most desirable dominant genes. A little small rabbit might make a nice pet for someone but if you want to produce a quality breeding stock then make sure that they meet these physical requirements/qualities because usually large healthy parents tend to produce healthy offspring.

How to Price Your Rabbits/ Rabbit Meat

Before putting your rabbits up for sale it is important to decide for a reasonable price. You can price them based upon the cost of feed and the value of your effort. As like any other business or hobby at first you may be forced to work without much monetary compensation. The important thing is that you enjoy your new hobby and or business. It's also highly recommended that you take into consideration the value of the knowledge that you have learned from your rabbit project in determining the price.

Many rabbit raisers price their breeding stock at around $60 - $100 each. Usually the rabbits sell at around $50 and the rabbit meat is based on the average market price. It's also recommended that you price your average breeding stock somewhere between $40 - $100 each. If you have a rare or giant breed or simply have a really excellent rabbit breed for sale, then you can probably charge higher but make sure that you keep your average prices in this range for a breeding stock.

In general though, pet rabbits can usually be sold for around $30 - $100 each (depending upon breed, quality and rarity). On the other hand, meat rabbits generally need to be sold at an average market price or else nobody will buy them. Meat buyers usually pay between $1 - 1.75 per pound of live rabbit.

Of course, the prices mentioned are just a guide for you. You can charge whatever prices you wish and can sell as many animals as the market will buy. It may be best to consider the recommended average price because it will not only help you sell more rabbits but it will also help you acquire a good reputation. If you do things right you can still make a decent profit without overcharging your market.

How to Gain Good Reputation

When you are running any type of business it is important to develop a good reputation amongst customers and potential buyers. Here are some tips which will help you develop a good reputation as a rabbit raiser:

- Offer reasonable prices
- Be sure to help your customers get started with their rabbit adventure
- Answer questions that your customers send you to the best of your ability
- Give your customers an honest evaluation of the rabbits that you are selling them
- Show kindness to others
- Attend any local rabbit meetings or clinics around your area so you can meet other rabbit enthusiasts and gain more knowledge
- Have a great time raising these cute bunnies

Additional Rabbit Revenue Streams

It is always nice to be able to make additional revenue off of your rabbit project even if you are only into rabbit raising for a hobby. There are two ways you can do to increase your revenues when it comes to raising rabbits. You can sell their manure or sell it as fertilizers and/or grow your own worms under rabbit hutches, then sell it as fish bait.

You can sell your rabbit manure as plant fertilizer because rabbit manure is by far one of the most valuable types of fertilizer in the world! The reason for this is because rabbit food is high in protein and quality which results in the natural development of a very high quality rabbit manure. Rabbit fertilizer is valuable to people who plant gardens and it even works great if you apply it to orchards according to most rabbit enthusiasts.

Ways on How to Market Your Rabbits

Business Cards

There are something's that never die! And when it comes to business and marketing – you might still want to consider giving out business cards like a real entrepreneur! You should never underestimate the effectiveness of business cards if you are serious about creating a rabbit enterprise, and with today's technology you can make it in just a few minutes by using programs like Microsoft Publisher or automatic app creators to create business cards for your rabbitry.

It's also highly recommended that you always give 3 pieces of business cards to people because if your customers or potential buyers are happy with their rabbits, there's a huge chance that they will end up giving out these cards to their friends.

Flyer Promotion

Flyers are another great way to find customers locally. Type up some rabbitry flyers in a program such as Microsoft Publisher or online apps, and do it the old fashion way by simply hanging these flyers up on local bulletin boards. You might just be surprised how many people still glance at these boards! The best place to distribute flyers is at your local feed store or during pet conventions. Many people will check these places when they are in search of livestock or pets.

It's best that you connect with people during conventions because who knows? These people can help you locate buyers in your area and recommend potential customers to your rabbitry. Be sure to give these people at least one of your flyers or business cards.

Word of Mouth or Referral

Many entrepreneurs in every industry will agree that when it comes to marketing, nothing beats word of mouth or the referral system! If you have lived in the same town for quite some time, then you already know some people who would be willing to buy rabbits for either meat or pets. If you process your rabbits yourself, there could be plenty of locals who will be willing to order rabbit meat from you. Just ask around, and tell your friends to ask their friends and let those friends or previous customers spread the word! Doing this type of promotion will make you bound to run into potential customers or friends who know potential customers!

Website/Social Media

Relying on old – fashion marketing could help you reach local customers, but if you also use the power of internet marketing through setting up websites or social media pages you can potentially reach more customers, expand your business, and earn more profit with just a click of a button!

Websites and social media pages are a great way to reach out to potential customers in any state or even in other far – flung places. The great part is that it's easy to do it, and free! There is also another great way to reach potential customers online through using official rabbit platforms like sellrabbitsondemand.com or rabbitbreeders.us. You can simply post an ad for free (or sometimes for a minimum amount) so you can reach customers who are ready to buy already.

More Tips on How to Reach Your Potential Customers

- Make sure to place your phone number or email address on your business card/website/social media page/flyers/ online ads etc. If you have a website URL, be sure to put that on the promotional material too. However, make certain that buyers have an alternate way to contact you other than through the internet.

- It is a good idea to distribute your home phone number instead of your cell number on your promotional material/s or website. Ideally if you have a fulltime rabbit business you will have your own business phone number but if you don't, then just put your home phone number instead or perhaps a public cellphone number.

- Email is another good way to communicate with potential customers online. In fact, most breeder directories including rabbitbreeders.us list the email addresses of rabbit breeders on the listing pages.

- Make sure to make a special email address for your rabbitry business. You can go to gmail.com and create a free email account. If you ever change email addresses, instead of trying to update your breeder listings and promotional material then you can just forward the messages to your new email address for less hassle.

Chapter Ten: Care Sheet and Summary

Now that you have basic knowledge on how to take care of a Jersey Wooly, it's time for you to apply it, and of course get to learn new things! You can search online for more info about the breed or some additional info on how to make them healthy and happy as well as read more articles on how you can become a potentially reputable breeder.

In this chapter, we will give you the quick summary of the major points you need to remember that was discussed in this book. A quick glance can be of help if you are in a hurry or if you simply wanted to review something important.

Biological Information

Taxonomy: Kingdom *Animalia*, Phylum *Chordata*, Class *Mammalia*, Order *Lagomorpha*, Family *Leporidae*, and Genus *Oryctolagus*, *Oryctolagus cuniculus* species.

Country of Origin: New Jersey, United States

Breed Size: dwarf – size breed

Body Type and Appearance: Has a relatively small face with short hairs on it. The ears are also short but erect, and its wooly fluff goes through their whole body.

Weight: 1 to 3 pounds for both bucks and does, with 3 ½ pounds being the maximum senior weight

Coat Length: wooly coat

Coat Texture: dense, coarse, soft

Color: chestnut, squirrel color, chinchilla, and opal, lilac, blue, chocolate, black, blue – eyed – white, and red – eyed – white, smoke pearl, seal, Siamese sable, sable point tortoise shell, and blue tortoise shell, black and blue otter, sable marten, lilac silver marten, black silver marten, and chocolate silver marten, pointed white black, pointed white blue variety

Temperament: extremely docile, gentle, friendly, playful, sociable, trainable

Strangers: friendly around strangers

Other Rabbits: generally good with other rabbit breeds if properly introduced, trained, and socialized.

Other Pets: generally friendly with other pets but shouldn't be left with other huge animals because it might get scared since rabbits are mostly prey animals.

Other Names: "No - kick bunny," "mug head"

The Rabbit Buying Process

Where to Purchase Rabbits: Pet shops, flea markets, rabbit rescue centers, backyard rabbit breeders, rabbit hobbyists

Legal Requirements:

United States: In many cases, a license or permit is only required for exotic or endangered animals, fortunately Jersey Wooly rabbits do not qualify. There are, however, some local regulations which may require you to license your rabbit.

United Kingdom: Rabbit owners are not required to obtain a license or permit but if you plan to import a rabbit from outside the U.K. or export one outside the country, you will need to obtain an Animal Movement License (AML).

If you plan to sell your rabbits: Generally your business must be licensed unless you are only selling rabbits for meat or fiber. If you sell rabbits as pets, you do not need a license if your annual sales are under a certain revenue amount set by your state

Traits of a Reputable Rabbit Breeder:

Trait #1: Reputable rabbit breeders know their material

Trait #2: Reputable rabbit breeders are willing to provide assistance to the potential buyers

Trait #3: Reputable rabbit breeders will also ask about you or your reasons for keeping or caring a rabbit

Trait #4: Reputable rabbit breeders obviously have good reputation

Trait #5: Reputable rabbit breeders gives a health guarantee or has a contract

Selecting a Healthy Breed:

- Examine its body to make sure that there aren't any signs of health issues, injuries or inadequate living condition. Make sure the eyes, ears and snout have no discharge, and must be clear and clean. The body should be proportional and free of any health problems/injuries, and it should walk or hop normally without any sign of immobility.

Major Pro: Grooming will not be a problem because their wools are easy to brush and they don't shed as much like other rabbit breeds

Major Cons: They may not want to be touch or handled all the time. Although they can be laid back lap bunnies, they may get stress if they are always being handled.

Housing and Maintenance Requirements

Housing Guidelines and Hutch Materials

- Jersey wool rabbits are quite active animals which is why its cage should be large enough so that he can move around with ease.
- The cage itself should provide at least eight square feet of space for one or more rabbits.
- Make sure to buy a fresh hay bedding, durable hay feeder, stainless water and food dishes, litter pan, and stimulating toys as well as other decorations for your rabbit's cage.

Do – It - Yourself Rabbit Cage

Step 1: Decide on a cage type and the kind of material you want to use. You can choose to make a wire cage but make sure that the flooring has a mat or a covering to prevent irritation of your rabbit's feet.

Step 2: Gather your Supplies. You can normally find wire available at your local feed or hardware store

Step 3: Begin Building. Bend the wire around the corner of the wooden 2 by 4 to create the two 3 foot and 2 ½ foot sides.

Step 4: Finish the Sides. You should attach a clip about every 3 inches on the side.

Step 5: Attach the Bottom. Attach the ½ inch by 1 inch mesh wire piece to the sides

Step 6: Attach the Top. Attached the bottom attach the 1 inch by 2 inch mesh wire piece to form the top of the cage.

Step 7: Build the Door. Cut an opening of about 1 foot square on the wide side of the wire

Step 8: Decide on a Cage Location. Pick a spot on your rabbit's cage where you would like hay feeder to hang.

Step 9: Gather your materials (again). You will need to get out your pair of gloves and wire clippers to cutout the wire for the hay feeder.

Step 10: Start Constructing. Take the piece of wire and bend its two opposite sides into a rectangular U shape.

Step 11: Pay attention to details. Be sure to clip off any sharp edges on your hay rack.

Step 12: Attach the rack or hay feeder. Attach the new hay rack to your rabbit's cage

Step 13: Collect the dust. Place a piece of plastic under the hay rack to catch any dust that might fall through.

Feeding Your Jersey Wooly Rabbits

Rabbit Nutrition: Protein, Fiber, Fats

When and how to feed your rabbit:

- Most breeders recommend feeding rabbits at night because they are mostly active at night.
- Once a day feeding at night or early morning is appropriate.
- Make sure that your rabbit has access to fresh water supply all the time by using an automatic watering system.

Highly recommended food brands for rabbits: Petrus, Purina, Manna Pro, and Sherwood Forest Natural Rabbit Food

Rabbit Feeding Tips:

- Feed your rabbits some type of hay on a frequent basis
- The most effective rabbit food is a nice pellet based feed with veggies and fruits from time to time
- When buying rabbits from a breeder, be sure to ask them the brand of food they gave to your rabbit so that there will be consistency

Rabbit Husbandry

How to Remove a Rabbit from its Cage:

- Your palms should be place in your pet's abdomen; once you do that's when you lift them up.
- If your pet struggle or isn't comfortable you can use your other hand to support the shoulders and/or grip its skin.
- Once you have lifted it out of the cage, you should provide support to its legs using your hand or lean it over your body.

How to Carry a Rabbit:

- Hold your pet's ears and its shoulders in your right hand while placing its feet on your left arm

- Support your rabbit's rear with your left hand
- Finally tuck your Jersey wooly's head under your left elbow

Grooming

- When it comes to grooming, you'll have no problem maintaining your Jersey Wooly's fur because even if its coat is dense, it is very easy to brush. In fact, you don't really need to brush it daily, you can however brush it once or twice a week to maintain its beautiful fur and avoid any debris on its coat.
- Most rabbits hate getting wet and that includes your Jersey Wooly!
- When trimming your rabbit's nails, it is best to just trim off the sharp tip.
- In order to clean your Jersey Wooly's ears, just dip a cotton ball in a mild antiseptic solution and squeeze out any excess liquid.
- When it comes to your rabbit's teeth, you should make sure that it is checked by a veterinarian at least twice a year

Breeding Your Jersey Wooly Rabbit

Reasons to Breed Rabbits

- The process of raising and caring for baby bunnies can be a fun and interesting learning experience
- Rabbit breeding can be a profitable business

Things to Consider Before Breeding

- Bunnies will grow up quickly and require more space (so be prepared)
- You will need to purchase or make a nest box for each doe that you breed
- Successfully raising up bunny rabbits will require a dedication of time and labor

Rabbit breeding season or cycle: As long as you have a healthy doe and an eager buck, cycles or breeding seasons don't really matter. In fact, some female rabbits living in the wild will get pregnant up to eight times a year.

Ideal season to breed Jersey Wooly: The ideal seasons to breed your pet rabbits are spring, fall and winter.

Rabbit Breeding Schedule: In order to keep your rabbits in good breeding health you need to breed your rabbits at least three times a year.

Gestation Cycle: Jersey Wooly rabbits' gestation cycle take approximately 30 days from breeding to kindling.

Average litter size for Jersey Wooly: 3 – 4 bunnies

Do – It – Yourself Nesting Box

Step 1: Decide on a model. You can choose to build such as a wooden nest boxes, wood and wire nest boxes and all metal nest boxes.

Step 2: Buy the materials you need. One of the best things about wooden nest boxes is the fact that they are cheap and easy to make.

Step 3: Cut the plywood.

Step 4: Cutout an opening. You will need cutout a section of the board so that your rabbit can access the nest box

Step 5: Nailing time! The back board should be on top of the bottom board so that the height is even with the sides.

Step 6: Construction time! Set up the top board to rest on top of the other boards and make sure that it is aligned properly.

Step 7: The finishing touches. Finish drilling the screws into the sides of the board.

Showing Your Jersey Wooly Rabbit

Jersey Wooly Schedule of Points:

- General Type – 58
- Body – 30
- Head – 16
- Ears – 10
- Eyes – 2
- Feet and Legs – 0
- Wool – 27
- Texture – 14
- Density – 8
- Length – 5
- Color – 10
- Condition – 5

Total Points: 100

Showmanship Reminders:

- Registering your rabbit for a show is fairly easy but you want to make sure you don't overlook anything that might get you disqualified so start reading the rules and regulations for that specific show.

- Put together a kit of items that may come in handy on show day such as your rabbit's registration information, food and water, nail clippers, hydrogen peroxide (for cleaning injuries and spots on white coats), slicker brush and other grooming supplies, business cards, contact information, paper towels and wet wipes, scrap carpet square (for last minute grooming), extra clothes, food, and water for yourself.

Health Problems: Symptoms, Causes and Treatments

Bacterial Diseases

- Sniffles Disease
- Urine Scald
- Abscesses
- Pneumonia

Viral Diseases

- Viral Hemorrhagic Disease (RVHD)
- Infectious Myxomatosis

Fungal Diseases and External Parasitic Conditions

- Mange Mites
- Ringworm

- E. Cuniculi

Tips in Finding a Savvy Rabbit Veterinarian

- Ask for referral from your friends who are also rabbit keepers. Chances are they know a vet who is rabbit experts
- You can look at various rabbit organizations for a list of recommended rabbit vets. These vets applied to be on the recommended list and were approved by these organizations which mean that they somehow pass the standards.

Marketing Your Rabbits

Common Problem in Marketing or Selling Rabbits

- Breeding rabbits are often crowded into hutches due to herd overpopulation which may result in spread of illnesses or become stressful for the rabbits.
- Many times herd overpopulation leads to another problem such as poor herd management.

Qualities of a Reputable Rabbitry

- The place or facility should be clean and well organized

- The rabbits should have hutches of their own to reside in and to avoid being crowded

How to Earn to Money Off of Rabbits

Selling Live Rabbit: The easiest way to cover rabbitry expenses is to sell live rabbit meat to local markets or people who like to purchase or eat rabbit meat.

Selling Rabbit Meat Packages: If you are desperate to get rid of rabbits the best option for you might be to slaughter and process the rabbits yourself, and then sell the meat.

Selling to a laboratory market: Once you have become an established rabbit breeder with a good reputation and/or large herd you might just be able to sell some of your excess stock to a laboratory market to test out skin products that are made for humans

Pet Market: The rabbit pet market has grown big time, so if you are raiser who breeds many small to medium size rabbit breeds this is a good option to earn revenue.

Qualities of a Great Breeding Stock Rabbit

- The rabbits should remain healthy and would only require very little treatment
- The rabbits from a great breeding stock usually grows faster than the rest of the bunnies born in the litter

- The rabbit has a good body type

How to Gain Good Reputation

- Offer reasonable prices
- Be sure to help your customers get started with their rabbit adventure
- Answer questions that your customers send you to the best of your ability

Ways on How to Market Your Rabbits

- Business Cards
- Flyer Promotion
- Word of Mouth or Referral
- Website/Social Media

Glossary of Rabbit Terms

Agouti – A type of coloring in which the hair shaft has three or more bands of color with a definite break between.

Albino – A pink-eyed, white-furred rabbit.

ARBA – The American Rabbit Breeders Association; an organization which promotes rabbits in the United States.

Awn – The strong, straight guard hairs protruding above the undercoat in angora breeds.

Bangs – Longer fur appearing at the front base of the ears and on top of the head in some woolen breeds.

Base Color – The color of the fur next to the skin.

Bell Ears – Ears that have large tips with distinct fall.

Belt – The line where the colored portion of the coat meets the white portion, just behind the shoulders.

Blaze – A white marking found on the head of the Dutch rabbit; the shape is wedge-like.

Bonding – A term used to describe two rabbits that have paired up together.

BRC – The British Rabbit Council, formed from the British Rabbit Society and the National Rabbit Council of Great Britain in 1934.

Broken Coat – Guard hairs that are missing or broken in places, exposing the undercoat.

Buck – An intact male rabbit.

Buff – A rich, golden-orange color.

Caecotroph – Pellets of semi-digested food eaten from the anus for nutrition reasons.

Chinning – Rubbing the chin on objects of people to spread scent from glands under the chin.

Cobby – A term meaning stout or stocky in body; short legs.

Condition – The overall physical state of a rabbit in terms of its fur, health, cleanliness, and grooming.

Crossbreeding – Mating two different breeds.

Cull – The process of selecting the best rabbits from a litter and selling or slaughtering the rest.

Dam – A female rabbit that has produced offspring.

Doe – An unaltered female rabbit.

Flat Coat – Fur lying too close to the body, lacking spring and body as noted by touch.

Fryer – A young meat rabbit no more than 10 weeks of age and weighing less than 5 pounds.

Gestation – The period of time between breeding and birthing (or kindling).

Guard Hair – The long, coarser hairs in a rabbit's coat which protect the undercoat.

Herd – A group of rabbits.

Inbreeding – Breeding of closely related stock.

Junior – A class of rabbits referring to those under 6 months of age.

Kindling – The process of giving birth to baby rabbits (kits).

Kindling Box – A box provided for a pregnant rabbit so she can make a nest and give birth.

Kit – A baby rabbit.

Line Breeding – A breeding program in which rabbits that are descended from the same animal are bred.

Litter – A group of young rabbits born to one doe at the same time.

Loose Coat – Fur conditions in the undercoat, often coupled with smooth hair resulting in not so good texture.

Malocclusion – A misalignment of the rabbit's teeth.

Molt – The process of shedding or changing the fur, happens twice each year.

Nest Box – A box provided for a pregnant rabbit so she can make a nest and give birth.

Nursing – The process of kits suckling milk from the dam's teats; usually occurs twice a day.

Peanut – A rabbit with two dwarf genes; usually fatal.

Pelage – The fur coat or covering in a rabbit.

Pellets – May refer either to the rabbit's poop or its food.

Quick – The pink part of the nails/claws that contains the blood vessels and nerves.

Racy – Referring to a slim, slender body and legs.

Saddle – The rounded portion of the back between the rabbit's shoulder and loin.

Self-Colored – A fur pattern where the hair colors are the same all over the body.

Sire – A male rabbit that has produced offspring.

Thumping – The practice of banging or stomping the hind legs on the ground to make a loud, thudding noise.

Ticking - A wavy distribution of longer guard hairs throughout the rabbit's coat.

Weaning – The process in which baby rabbits become independent of their dam, transitioning to solid food.

Wool – A term used to describe the fur of Angora rabbits

Index

C

D

E

V

W

Photo Credits

Page 67 Photo by user vjmarisphotos via Flickr.com, https://www.flickr.com/photos/purduepics/7979677341/

Page 80 Photo by user vjmarisphotos via Flickr.com, https://www.flickr.com/photos/purduepics/7785487034/

Page 90 Photo by user Clement via Flickr.com, https://www.flickr.com/photos/k-ribou/6225375647/

References

"Basics of Breeding Rabbits"
ThreeLittleLadiesRabbitry.com

http://www.threelittleladiesrabbitry.com/breedingindex.php

"Bunny Breed Guide Jersey Woolly Rabbits"
Pethelpful.com

https://pethelpful.com/rabbits/Bunny-Breed-Guide-Jersey-Woolly-Rabbits

"Choosing a Jersey Wooly Rabbit" Petplace.com

http://www.petplace.com/article/small-mammals/general/small-mammal-profiles/choosing-a-jersey-wooly-rabbit

"Feeding Your Rabbit" CaringPets.org

https://www.caringpets.org/how-to-take-care-of-a-rabbit/#food-diet

"How to Build a Rabbit Hutch" CaringPets.org

https://www.caringpets.org/how-to-take-care-of-a-rabbit/how-to-build-a-house/

"How to Care for a Jersey Wooly Rabbit" Second – Opinion Doctor

http://www.second-opinion-doc.com/how-to-care-for-a-jersey-wooly-rabbit.html

"How to Groom Your Jersey Wooly" Jersey Wooly Rabbit Care

http://jerseywoolyrabbitcare.blogspot.com/

"Jersey Wooly" Petguide.com

http://www.petguide.com/breeds/rabbit/jersey-wooly/

"Jersey Wooly" Wikipedia.org

https://en.wikipedia.org/wiki/Jersey_Wooly

"Jersey Wooly Rabbits" Rabbit Breeders
http://rabbitbreeders.us/jersey-wooly-rabbits

"Jersey Wooly: Rabbit Breed Information" The Nature Trail

http://www.thenaturetrail.com/rabbit-breeds/jersey-wooly-rabbit-breed-information/

"Jersey Wooly Q & A" Fancy Furs

http://fancyfurs.weebly.com/jersey-wooly-qa.html

"Raising Angora Rabbits For Wool" The Spruce

https://www.thespruce.com/raising-angora-rabbits-for-wool-1835776

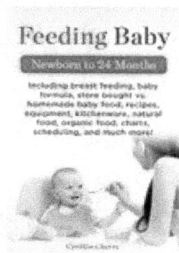

Feeding Baby
Cynthia Cherry
978-1941070000

Axolotl
Lolly Brown
978-0989658430

Dysautonomia, POTS
Syndrome
Frederick Earlstein
978-0989658485

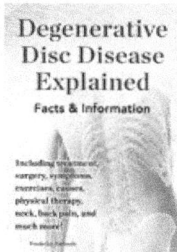

Degenerative Disc
Disease Explained
Frederick Earlstein
978-0989658485

Sinusitis, Hay Fever,
Allergic Rhinitis Explained
Frederick Earlstein
978-1941070024

Wicca
Riley Star
978-1941070130

Zombie Apocalypse
Rex Cutty
978-1941070154

Capybara
Lolly Brown
978-1941070062

Eels As Pets
Lolly Brown
978-1941070167

Scabies and Lice Explained
Frederick Earlstein
978-1941070017

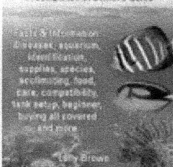

Saltwater Fish As Pets
Lolly Brown
978-0989658461

Torticollis Explained
Frederick Earlstein
978-1941070055

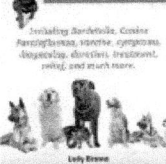

Kennel Cough
Lolly Brown
978-0989658409

Physiotherapist, Physical Therapist
Christopher Wright
978-0989658492

Rats, Mice, and Dormice As Pets
Lolly Brown
978-1941070079

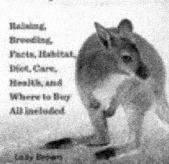

Wallaby and Wallaroo Care
Lolly Brown
978-1941070031

Bodybuilding Supplements
Explained
Jon Shelton
978-1941070239

Demonology
Riley Star
978-19401070314

Pigeon Racing
Lolly Brown
978-1941070307

Dwarf Hamster
Lolly Brown
978-1941070390

Cryptozoology
Rex Cutty
978-1941070406

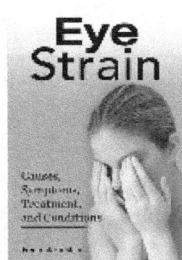

Eye Strain
Frederick Earlstein
978-1941070369

Inez The Miniature Elephant
Asher Ray
978-1941070353

Vampire Apocalypse
Rex Cutty
978-1941070321

www.ingramcontent.com/pod-product-compliance
Lightning Source LLC
LaVergne TN
LVHW051643080426
835511LV00016B/2469